Exposing
And
Conquering Social
Media Deceivers

Dion M. Blake

Table of Contents

Chapter One

The Ascent of Online Entertainment Duplicity

Figuring out the Multiplication of Tricksters

In the present computerized age, the multiplication of tricksters has turned into a major problem that influences people, organizations, and society all in all. Tricksters utilize different strategies to mislead and dupe clueless casualties, hurting. To battle this developing issue, it's significant to comprehend the explanations for the multiplication of tricksters and the systems they utilize.

Namelessness and the Web:

The web has given con artists a remarkable stage to work from, empowering them to remain to a great extent mysterious. They can make counterfeit personalities, sites, and email accounts, making it provoking for police to track them down. The secrecy given by the computerized world permits tricksters to work with the relative exemption.

Innovation Headways:

Headways in innovation have made it more straightforward for tricksters to contact a more extensive crowd. Devices like Voice over Web Convention (VoIP) permit tricksters to settle on telephone decisions from any place on the planet with a phony guest ID. Besides, complex programming can robotize misleading cycles, making it conceivable to all the while focusing on different casualties.

Social Designing:

Tricksters frequently utilize mental control procedures known as friendly designing. They exploit human feelings, like apprehension, avarice, and trust, to persuade their casualties to make moves that benefit the con artist. These strategies are profoundly powerful in misdirecting even the most mindful people.

Monetary Motivating Forces:

Monetary profit is an essential inspiration for tricksters. Tricks can be exceptionally rewarding, and for however long there are weak people or associations, con artists will keep on taking advantage of them for benefit. The commitment to income sans work draws in both beginner and expert tricksters.

Globalization:

The computerized age has worked with a globalized economy, making it simpler for tricksters to work across borders. Tricks starting in one nation can target casualties around the world. This worldwide aspect adds intricacy to policing, as jurisdictional limits become obscured.

Okay, High Prize:

Con artists frequently see their exercises as okay, high-reward tries. The possibilities of getting found out and arraigned are generally low contrasted with the likely monetary profits. This view of negligible results urges more people to participate in misleading.

Insufficient Schooling and Mindfulness:

Many individuals succumb to tricks because of an absence of training and mindfulness. Con artists continually adjust their strategies, making it provoking for people to remain informed about new dangers. An absence of computerized education can leave people defenseless against different web-based tricks.

Ineffectual Regulation:

Regulation frequently battles to stay aware of the quickly advancing strategies utilized by con artists. A few nations might miss the mark on the legitimate structure to address cybercrimes sufficiently, prompting holes in requirements and indictment.

Human Weakness:

Eventually, tricksters exploit the weaknesses of human brain science. They go after our trust, interest, and craving for monetary profit, making it urgent for people to stay watchful and incredulous while managing new web-based offers or demands.

Understanding the multiplication of tricksters is fundamental for creating successful procedures to battle this issue. It requires a complex methodology that incorporates upgraded instruction and mindfulness, further developed regulation, better worldwide collaboration, and continuous endeavors to remain in front of tricksters' advancing strategies. By tending to these underlying drivers, society can more readily shield people and associations from succumbing to tricks and decrease the general effect of con artists on our advanced world.

Kinds of Virtual Entertainment Double dealing

Virtual entertainment stages have turned into a fundamental piece of our regular routines, offering valuable open doors for association, correspondence, and self-articulation. Notwithstanding, they have additionally become favorable places for different types of misdirection. These trickeries range from innocuous embellishments to malevolent plans pointed toward controlling and taking advantage of clients. To explore the advanced scene securely, it's fundamental to comprehend the various kinds of web-based entertainment duplicity that can be experienced.

Duping:

Duping is the point at which somebody makes a phony web-based persona, frequently utilizing taken photographs and data, to mislead others into thinking they are another person. This tricky practice can prompt close-to-home control, online connections based on falsehoods, or even monetary tricks.

Counterfeit Profiles:

Counterfeit profiles are not generally made with malevolent expectations. A few people make them to keep up with security or for diversion. Notwithstanding, others utilize counterfeit profiles for duplicity, spreading deception, or taking part in cyberbullying.

Pantomime:

Pantomime happens when somebody professes to be someone else, frequently an individual of note or superstar. This type of trickery is normally expected for parody, spoof, or to delude others because of multiple factors. It tends to be deluding and destructive whenever treated seriously.

Misleading Content and Emotionalism:

Numerous web-based entertainment clients experience misleading content, which includes electrifying or misdirecting titles or pictures to bait clients into tapping on a connection or post. Misleading content is regularly used to produce promotion income or increment site traffic, frequently frustrating clients with immaterial or inferior quality substance.

Photoshopped or Adjusted Pictures:

Individuals frequently alter or control pictures via virtual entertainment to upgrade their appearance or make a specific picture. This type of double-dealing can prompt ridiculous magnificence norms and self-perception issues, as well as the spread of misleading data.

Counterfeit News and Deception:

The spread of phony news and deception via web-based entertainment is a huge concern. Tricky entertainers make and offer misleading data to control general assessment, sow dissension, or advance a specific plan. Falsehood can have expansive results, from affecting races to causing general well-being emergencies.

Phishing Tricks:

Phishing tricks include fooling people into uncovering individual data, for example, login certifications or monetary subtleties, through counterfeit online entertainment records or connections. These tricks are much of the time camouflaged as real messages from companions or confided in sources.

Force to be reckoned with Trickery:

A few online entertainment powerhouses might take part in tricky practices, for example, advancing items or administrations without uncovering their monetary advantages or utilizing channels and altering to introduce a glorified picture that is a long way from the real world.

Cyberbullying:

Cyberbullying includes utilizing virtual entertainment stages to irritate, compromise, or scare others. It can take many structures, including spreading misleading bits of gossip, slanderous remarks, or sharing confidential data without assent.

Online entertainment trickiness exists in different structures and levels of seriousness, going from moderately innocuous misrepresentations to vindictive tricks and provocation. As clients of online entertainment stages, it's fundamental to stay careful, assess data, and report misleading or destructive substances. Stages themselves are likewise attempting to battle these issues by executing arrangements, calculations, and announcing instruments to diminish the spread of double-dealing and safeguard clients from hurt. Instruction and mindfulness about the kinds of web-based entertainment trickery are pivotal for cultivating a more secure internet-based climate.

The Effect on People and Networks: Virtual Entertainment Trickiness

The expansion of web-based entertainment trickiness, as examined in the past segment, has sweeping outcomes, for people as well as for whole networks and society in general. This article investigates the significant effect of virtual entertainment trickiness on people and networks, digging into the profound, mental, and social outcomes it can have.

Influence on People

Profound Pain: People who succumb to trickery, whether through duping, cyberbullying, or falsehood, frequently experience close-to-home trouble. Sensations of embarrassment, treachery, and tension can come about because of finding that one has been misdirected or controlled on the web.

Emotional well-being: Misleading web-based encounters can add to psychological well-being issues, including misery and uneasiness. Cyberbullying, specifically, has been connected to negative psychological wellness results in casualties, prompting low confidence and, in extreme cases, self-hurt or self-destructive ideation.

Trust Issues: Trickiness via web-based entertainment can disintegrate trust in web-based communications. People might turn out to be more suspicious and careful, making it trying to shape certified associations in a computerized world that depends on trust.

Protection Concerns: The openness to different types of trickiness can make people more worried about their web-based protection and security. They might become reluctant to share individual data or connect straightforwardly via online entertainment.

Influence on Networks

Disintegration of Trust: Far and wide virtual entertainment misdirection can dissolve trust inside networks and society in general. At the point when individuals can't recognize truth from misrepresentation, trust in foundations, news sources, and, surprisingly, each other can decline.

Polarization: The spread of phony news and falsehood via virtual entertainment can add to the polarization of networks. Misleading stories can support existing convictions and make protected, closed-off environments, making it hard for individuals to participate in productive exchange and figure out something worth agreeing on.

Social Division: Misleading practices, like pantomime and online badgering, can prompt social division inside networks. Online contentions can gush out over into genuine circumstances, causing breaks among companions, families, and, surprisingly, whole networks.

General Wellbeing Results: Falsehood about wellbeing-related issues, as seen during the Coronavirus pandemic, can have extreme general well-being outcomes. Networks might be more defenseless to the spread of sicknesses and less inclined to embrace preventive measures because of misleading data.

Financial Effect: People groups that depend vigorously on the web for business and trade can experience monetary misfortunes because of online trickery. Phishing tricks, for instance, can prompt monetary misfortunes for people and organizations the same.

The effect of web-based entertainment duplicity on people and networks is intricate and multi-layered. It reaches out past private feelings to include more extensive social and monetary results. Resolving this issue requires a blend of individual watchfulness, stage guidelines, media education projects, and aggregate endeavors to advance truth and straightforwardness in web-based connections. By perceiving and moderating the adverse consequences of virtual entertainment double-dealing, people and networks can pursue cultivating a more secure, confiding web-based climate.

Chapter Two

Perceiving the Warnings

Distinguishing Normal Trickster Strategies

Tricksters utilize a wide exhibit of strategies to delude people and associations. Having the option to recognize these normal trickster strategies is vital for protecting yourself and your resources in the present computerized age. In this article, we will investigate the absolute most predominant strategies utilized by tricksters to help you perceive and try not to succumb to their plans.

Phishing Messages and Messages:

Phishing is one of the most pervasive con artist strategies. Con artists send misleading messages or messages that seem, by all accounts, to be from confided-in sources, similar to banks, virtual entertainment stages, or government offices. They frequently ask beneficiaries to tap on joins or download connections, which can prompt malware establishment or the robbery of individual data.

Warnings: Be mindful of startling messages mentioning individual or monetary data, linguistic mistakes, nonexclusive good tidings, and emails tend to that don't match the authority space.

Pantomime:

Tricksters might imitate authentic people or associations to acquire trust and control casualties. They frequently claim to be technical support, government authorities, or even loved ones in trouble.

Warnings: Check the character of the individual or association through true channels, try not to share individual data without affirmation, and be careful about spontaneous solicitations for cash or help.

Counterfeit Sites and Mocking:

Tricksters make false sites that copy real ones, frequently with slight varieties in the URL. These phony locales are utilized for gathering login accreditations and visa data, or to circulate malware.

Warnings: Cautiously look at site URLs for incorrect spellings, and strange area augmentations, and guarantee the site utilizes secure HTTPS encryption.

Unrealistic Offers:

Con artists tempt casualties with offers that appear to be too great to even think about missing, for example, fantastic limits, lottery wins, or easy money scams. They mean to take advantage of individuals' covetousness or longing for income sans work.

Warnings: Exercise suspicion when offers appear to be unrealistic. Do all necessary investigation, and assuming that something sounds excessively simple or ridiculous, it likely is.

Close to home Control:

Con artists frequently utilize profound control to persuade casualties to act rapidly and automatically. They might take advantage of dread, culpability, or desperation to pressure people into pursuing rushed choices.

Warnings: Make a stride back when you feel constrained, and talk with confided-in companions or relatives before simply deciding on monetary exchanges.

Spontaneous Solicitations for Cash:

Con artists might contact people professing to be in desperate circumstances or crises, mentioning prompt monetary help. This strategy goes after compassion and a longing to help.

Warnings: Confirm the character of the individual making the solicitation through different means, and try not to send cash to obscure people without checking what is going on.

Excessive charge Tricks:

In different web-based exchanges, tricksters might send a check or installment surpassing the settled-upon sum and solicit the overabundance to be returned. Afterward, the underlying installment is viewed as false, leaving casualties with misfortunes.

Warnings: Be wary of excessive charge situations and never discount cash until you've confirmed the authenticity of the underlying installment.

Monitoring normal con artist strategies is the primary line of guard against succumbing to their plans. Make sure to pay attention to your gut feelings, lead an expected level of investment, and look for guidance from confided-in sources when confronted with dubious or spontaneous offers or demands. By remaining careful and informed, you can more readily safeguard yourself and your resources from con artists in the computerized age.

Indications of Dubious Online Entertainment Profiles

Online entertainment has turned into a fundamental piece of our lives, giving open doors to association, correspondence, and sharing. Notwithstanding, it has likewise turned into a ripe ground for the making of dubious or counterfeit profiles. Distinguishing these dubious profiles is fundamental to safeguarding yourself from tricks, badgering, and protection breaks. In this article, we will investigate the signs that can assist you with perceiving possibly dubious online entertainment profiles.

Inadequate or Nonexclusive Profile Data:

Dubious profiles frequently need point-by-point or legitimate data. Search for signs, for example, missing profile pictures, restricted individual subtleties, dubious or nonexclusive profiles, and conflicting or improbable data in the profile.

Restricted Action and Commitment:

Con artists frequently have restricted virtual entertainment action, with few posts, likes, or remarks. Their timetables might seem desolate or contain a couple of conventional posts. Furthermore, the shortfall of companions, supporters, or associations can be a warning.

An excessive number of Companions or Devotees in a Brief time frame:

A few phony profiles quickly gather an enormous number of companions or devotees in a brief period. On the off chance that a profile has a huge number of associations however little commitment or communication, it very well might be an indication of dubious movement.

Surprising or Tedious Substance:

Keep an eye out for profiles that share strange or redundant substance, for example, indistinguishable posts or pictures posted on numerous occasions. This could show a bot or a spam account.

Conflicting Language or Sentence Structure:

Numerous con artists work from locales where English isn't the essential language. Subsequently, their profiles might show conflicting language utilization or syntactic mistakes, especially in correspondence with likely casualties.

Demand for Individual Data:

Be careful on the off chance that a profile requests individual data, for example, your telephone number, address, or monetary subtleties, particularly assuming that it does so in a confidential message. Authentic people or associations for the most part don't demand touchy data immediately.

Dubious Connections and Offers:

Profiles that consistently share dubious connections offers that appear to be unrealistic, or advance sketchy items or administrations ought to be drawn closer with incredulity. These could be endeavors to take part in phishing or tricks.

No Common Associations:

If a profile has no common companions or associations with you and offers no normal interests or affiliations, it very well might be worth examining further.

Pantomime:

Check if the profile is mimicking another person, particularly a well-known person or a notable person. Pantomime records might utilize taken photographs and data to misdirect others.

Various Records with Comparative Names:

In some cases, tricksters make various phony profiles with comparative names and photographs. This strategy intends to mislead and control clients more.

Perceiving the indications of dubious web-based entertainment profiles is vital for keeping up with your web-based security and protection. Continuously practice mindfulness and incredulity while cooperating with new profiles. Assuming you experience a profile that raises doubts, report it to the web-based entertainment stage for additional examination and, when essential, do whatever it may take to safeguard your data and computerized presence. By remaining watchful, you can decrease the gamble of succumbing to tricks and different types of online misdirection.

Genuine Double-Dealing Stories

Genuine double-dealing stories act as wake-up calls, offering experiences of the intricate and frequently evil manners by which people and associations use trickiness to accomplish their goals. These accounts shed light on the intricacy of human brain science and the weaknesses that can be taken advantage of. In this article, we investigate some striking genuine double-dealing stories that stand out.

Elizabeth Holmes and Theranos:

One of the most high-profile instances of double-dealing as of late elaborate Elizabeth Holmes and her medical care innovation organization, Theranos. Holmes professed to have created a progressive blood-testing innovation that could play out a large number of tests with only a couple of drops of blood. Nonetheless, it was subsequently uncovered that the innovation didn't function as promoted, and Theranos had participated in a huge extortion to draw in financial backers and accomplices.

Bernie Madoff's Ponzi Plan:

Bernie Madoff coordinated perhaps the biggest monetary extortion in history through his Ponzi conspire. North of quite a few years, Madoff misdirected a large number of financial backers by promising reliably exceptional yields on their ventures. As a general rule, he was utilizing assets from new financial backers to pay back to prior financial backers. The plan fell in 2008, bringing about huge monetary misfortunes.

Anna Sorokin, the "Russian Beneficiary":

Anna Sorokin acted like a well-off Russian beneficiary in New York City, carrying on with an extravagant way of life and remaining in lavish lodgings without covering her bills. She persuaded companions, organizations, and even banks to give her labor and products because of her alleged abundance. Sorokin's trickery prompted her to be indicted for various charges, including robbery of administrations.

The Fyre Celebration Catastrophe:

The Fyre Celebration was showcased as a rich live event in the Bahamas, highlighting top-level entertainers and extreme facilities. Notwithstanding, when participants showed up, they found shoddy offices, a lack of food, and tumultuous circumstances. The celebration's coordinators had utilized misleading communication and online entertainment forces to be reckoned with to make a tricky picture of the occasion, which at last prompted its disappointment and lawful repercussions.

Activity Varsity Blues:

In 2019, an embarrassment named "Activity Varsity Blues" uncovered a plan in which well-off guardians, including famous people and business pioneers, paid off school mentors and chairmen to tie down confirmation for their kids to esteemed colleges. The trickiness included manufactured athletic profiles and undermining state-administered tests.

The Enron Embarrassment:

The Enron embarrassment is one of the main corporate extortion cases ever. Chiefs at the Enron Enterprise participated in bookkeeping rehearses that covered the organization's monetary misfortunes while blowing up its benefits. Investors and workers were misled, bringing about gigantic monetary misfortunes and the possible liquidation of the organization.

Duping and Online Sentiment Tricks:

Endless people have succumbed to duping and online sentiment tricks. In these cases, people make counterfeit web-based personas to lay out close-to-home associations with casualties, frequently prompting demands for cash or different types of double-dealing. These accounts feature the close-to-home cost and monetary misfortunes that can result from online misdirection.

Genuine double-dealing stories act as strong tokens of the limit concerning deceitfulness and control in a human way of behaving. They highlight the significance of decisive reasoning, an expected level of investment, and wariness while assessing cases and valuable open doors. By gaining from these accounts, people and society can turn out to be stronger in double-dealing and better prepared to safeguard themselves from succumbing to tricks, fakes, and different types of untrustworthiness.

Chapter Three

Exposing the Con artists

Insightful Methods for Uncovering Double Crossers

Revealing backstabbers is a basic expertise in different fields, including policing, and network safety. Whether it includes uncovering fraudsters, uncovering stowed-away plans, or distinguishing falsehood crusades, analytical methods assume an urgent part in uncovering reality. In this chapter, we will investigate a few powerful insightful procedures for uncovering double-crossers.

Computerized Impression Investigation:

In the computerized age, people leave a significant computerized impression. Insightful experts can investigate online exercises, including web-based entertainment posts, email interchanges, and site cooperations. Examples of conduct, irregularities, or associations with other tricky exercises might arise.

Historical verifications:

Leading extensive personal investigations can uncover stowed-away data about people. This might include confirming schooling and business history, actually taking a look at criminal records, and inspecting monetary records for inconsistencies.

Reconnaissance and Stakeouts:

Actual reconnaissance and stakeouts are exemplary insightful methods. They can be utilized to screen people associated with misleading exercises, assemble proof, and uncover stowed-away plans.

Meetings and Cross examinations:

Talented questioners can utilize strategies to inspire data from people, in any event, when they are endeavoring to misdirect. This might incorporate utilizing affinity building, questions that could go either way and non-verbal signs to recognize irregularities in reactions.

Scientific Examination:

Scientific specialists can break down actual proof, like archives, monetary records, or advanced media, to reveal misdirection. This can include penmanship examination, legal bookkeeping, and advanced criminology to recognize altering or control.

Polygraph Assessments:

Polygraph assessments, regularly known as untruth identifier tests, measure physiological reactions, for example, pulse, circulatory strain, and sweat to evaluate honesty. While not idiot-proof, they can be a significant device in recognizing trickery.

Mental Profiling:

Clinicians and profilers can evaluate a singular's way of behaving, character, and inspirations to distinguish designs steady with misdirection. This approach can be particularly helpful in criminal examinations.

Covert Activities:

Spies or writers might invade tricky gatherings or associations to accumulate proof and uncover unlawful or dishonest exercises from the inside.

Informants and Witnesses:

People with insider information can give important data about tricky practices. Safeguarding informants and sources is urgent for getting their participation and guaranteeing their well-being.

Information Investigation and Example Acknowledgment:

Enormous scope information examination, frequently supported by AI calculations, can reveal dubious examples or peculiarities in monetary exchanges, correspondences, or conduct that might demonstrate trickery.

Open-Source Knowledge (OSINT):

OSINT includes gathering data from openly accessible sources, for example, web-based entertainment, news stories, and freely available reports. Gifted OSINT examiners can uncover important bits of knowledge about people or associations that took part in tricky exercises.

Joint Effort and Data Sharing:

Compelling examinations frequently include cooperation among different offices and specialists. Sharing data and assets can prompt more far-reaching and effective endeavors to uncover tricksters.

Uncovering swindlers requires a mix of customary insightful methods and current devices and approaches. It likewise requests a sharp comprehension of human brain research, conduct, and inspiration. These insightful strategies are fundamental for policing as well as for columnists, network safety experts, and anybody looking to uncover misdirection and safeguard themselves and their associations from false or misleading exercises.

Gathering Proof and Documentation

Gathering proof and documentation is an essential move toward different fields, including policing, procedures, insightful news-casting, and examination, and the sky is the limit from there. Precise and far-reaching proof structures the establishment for pursuing informed choices, tackling issues, and laying out reality. In this article, we will investigate the significance of get-together proof and documentation, alongside pragmatic strategies for doing so actually.

The Significance of Get-together Proof and Documentation

Laying out Reality: Proof and documentation act as a way to lay out what occurred or to check the precision of cases. In judicial actions, this is fundamental for accomplishing equity.

Supporting Cases: In examination, reporting, and different expert settings, proof gives validity and backing to cases, contentions, and discoveries. It improves the dependability of your work.

Critical thinking: Proof recognizes the underlying drivers of issues, empowering more viable arrangements. In fields like network safety, gathering proof is basic for understanding and relieving dangers.

Navigation: Successful dynamic depends on approaching important information and data. Gathering proof assists leaders with settling on informed decisions.

Down to earth Procedures for Get-together Proof and Documentation

Documentation:

Record Keeping: Keep up with intensive records of significant data, like dates, times, areas, and people included.

Photos and Recordings: Visual documentation can be strong proof. Use cameras or cell phones to catch pictures or recordings when material.

Meetings and Articulations

Witness Meetings: Converse with witnesses and archive their assertions precisely. Guarantee their assertions are marked and dated.

Well-qualified Suppositions: Counsel specialists in pertinent fields to give proficient conclusions or examinations.

Advanced Proof

Information Conservation: In computerized examinations, guarantee the safeguarding of computerized proof in a forensically sound way.

Metadata: Analyze metadata, which can give significant settings and validation to computerized documents.

Reconnaissance and Checking

Reconnaissance Cameras: Use observation cameras to catch ongoing proof in regions where it is lawfully and morally allowed.

Observing Programming: Utilize checking instruments for following and archiving advanced exercises, for example, network traffic or representative PC use.

Documentation Principles

Keep up with Precision: Guarantee that everything proof is reported precisely, without predisposition or change.

Chain of Guardianship: In lawful settings, keep an unmistakable chain of care for actual proof to guarantee its uprightness.

Substantiating Proof

Numerous Sources: Look for verifying proof from different sources to reinforce your case or contention.

Cross-Confirmation: Check data through autonomous means to limit the gamble of mistakes or misdirection.

Legitimate and Moral Contemplations

Comply with Regulations: Know about legitimate prerequisites and limitations connected with social occasion proof. Unlawfully acquired proof might be prohibited in court.

Regard Protection: Consistently regard people's security and privileges while gathering proof. Get assent where fundamental.

Record Your Cycle

System: Record the techniques and cycles used to accumulate proof. This helps other people get it and imitate your work.

Timestamps: Use timestamps to lay out the order of occasions and moves made.

Chain of Guardianship

Keep a Chain: In legitimate settings, keep a chain of care for actual proof to show that it has not been messed with.

Coordinated effort and Mastery

Counsel Specialists: While managing mind-boggling or concentrated proof, counsel specialists in the pertinent field for direction and examination.

Gathering proof and documentation is a crucial part of critical thinking, independent direction, and equity. It expects tender loving care, adherence to moral and legitimate guidelines, and the utilization of fitting devices and strategies. Whether you are engaged with policing, news-casting, or some other field, viable proof social occasion guarantees the exactness and believability of your work, prompting more educated and solid results.

Announcing Con Artists to Virtual Entertainment Stages

As online entertainment stages have become progressively famous, they have likewise turned into a favorable place for tricksters and false exercises. Detailing tricksters to these stages is a crucial stage in guaranteeing a more secure web-based climate for clients. In this article, we will investigate the significance of revealing tricksters and give a bit-by-bit guide on the most proficient method to report dubious or deceitful records on different virtual entertainment stages.

Why Report Con artists via Web-based Entertainment Stages:

Safeguarding Yourself As well as other people: Announcing con artists shields both you and different clients from succumbing to extortion, wholesale fraud, or provocation.

Forestalling Further Mischief: By revealing tricksters, you can keep them from proceeding with their misleading exercises and focusing on additional casualties.

Keeping up with Stage Trustworthiness: Detailing tricksters keep up with the honesty of the online entertainment stage, making it a more secure and pleasant spot for everybody.

Legitimate and Moral Obligation: Detailing criminal operations, like tricks or badgering, is both a lawful and moral obligation. It adds to a more secure and more mindful internet-based local area.

Instructions to Report Tricksters via Online Entertainment Stages

Here is a bit-by-bit guide on the best way to report dubious or fake records on probably the most famous virtual entertainment stages:

Facebook:

Go to the Con artist's Profile: Visit the profile of the trickster you need to report.

Click on the Three Dabs: On the con artist's profile page, click on the three spots (...) situated on the cover photograph.

Select "Find Backing or Report Profile": A drop-down menu will show up. Pick "Find Backing or Report Profile."

Adhere to the On-Screen Directions: Facebook will direct you through the revealing system. You can report different issues, like pantomime, provocation, or tricks. Give however much data as could be expected.

Twitter:

Visit the Con artist's Profile: Go to the profile of the trickster you need to report.

Click on the Three Specks: Snap on the three spots (more choices) situated on the right half of the profile's cover photograph.

Pick "Report": From the dropdown menu, select "Report."

Select the Justification behind Revealing: Twitter offers a few detailing choices, including spam, counterfeit records, badgering, or dubious substance. Pick the most suitable choice.

Instagram:

Visit the Con artist's Profile: Explore the profile of the trickster you need to report.

Tap on the Three Dabs: On the upper right corner of the profile, tap on the three spots (...).

Pick "Report": Select "Report" from the choices.

Follow the Revealing System: Instagram will direct you through the announcing system, where you can determine the justification behind detailing and give extra subtleties.

LinkedIn:

Visit the Con artist's Profile: Go to the trickster's LinkedIn profile.

Click on "More...": Snap on the "More..." button situated on the right half of the profile picture.

Select "Report/Block": Pick "Report/Block" from the dropdown menu.

Follow the Announcing System: LinkedIn will provoke you to determine the justification behind revealing and give more subtleties.

Recall that different online entertainment stages might have somewhat unique announcing strategies. Continuously adhere to the stage explicit guidelines given during the revealing system.

Detailing tricksters to web-based entertainment stages is a fundamental stage in guaranteeing a more secure internet-based climate. By instantly announcing dubious or deceitful records, you add to the stage's endeavors to battle tricks and shield clients from trickery and mischief. Your activities can have a tremendous effect on keeping up with the honesty and security of online networks.

Chapter Four

Defending Your Internet-based Presence

Fortifying Your Protection Settings

In the present computerized world, safeguarding your web-based protection is of central significance. Reinforcing your security settings on different web-based stages is a proactive measure to protect your data and computerized character. In this article, we will investigate why protection settings matter and give aid on the best way to improve them on famous internet-based stages.

Why Fortify Your Security Settings

Safeguarding Individual Data: Solid security settings assist with forestalling unapproved admittance to your information, including your contact data, photographs, and posts.

Limit Information Openness: By restricting what you share freely, you decrease the gamble of data fraud, tricks, and undesirable requests.

Forestall Undesirable Contact: Security settings can assist you with controlling who can message or follow you, decreasing spam and provocation.

Keep up with Notoriety: Dealing with your internet-based presence through protection settings guarantees that your advanced character lines up with your genuine persona.

Protect Against: Areas of strength for cyberbullying settings can keep cyberbullies from focusing on you or your friends and family.

Safeguard Individual and Monetary Security: Upgraded protection settings can assist with defending touchy data that could be taken advantage of by con artists or lawbreakers.

Instructions to Reinforce Your Protection Settings:

Here is a bit-by-bit manual for improving protection settings on well-known web-based stages:

1. Facebook:

Click the descending confronting bolt in the upper right corner.

Select "Settings and Protection," then, at that point "Security Exam."

Survey your security settings for posts, profile data, and applications.

Change settings to your ideal degree of security.

2. Twitter:

Click on your profile picture, then, at that point "Settings and security."

Explore the "Security and wellbeing" segment.

Audit settings for tweets, security, and well-being, and make changes appropriately.

3. Instagram:

Open your profile and tap the three level lines (menu) on the upper right.

Go to "Settings" > "Protection."

Survey and change settings for account protection, associations, and information use.

4. LinkedIn:

Click on your profile picture and select "Settings and Protection."

Survey settings connected with protection, information, and security.

Alter settings in light of your inclinations.

5. Gmail:

Open Gmail and click on the stuff symbol (Settings) in the upper right corner.

Select "See all settings."

Survey your general and security settings, including two-factor verification and protection controls.

6. Cell phones:

Set up screen locks (PIN, secret word, unique mark, facial acknowledgment) to safeguard your gadget.

Survey application consents and limits admittance to delicate information.

Empower gadget encryption and remote wipe if there should be an occurrence of misfortune or burglary.

7. Internet Browsers:

Redo your program's security settings, like obstructing outsider threats or utilizing secret/confidential perusing modes.

Introduce security-centered program augmentations, similar to promotion blockers and trackers.

8. Online Administrations:

Audit and change protection settings for different internet-based administrations, including distributed storage, email, and online entertainment.

Empower two-factor verification at every possible opportunity.

9. Consistently Update Protection Settings:

Intermittently return to your protection settings to guarantee they line up with your ongoing inclinations.

Remain informed about stage refreshes and new security highlights.

Reinforcing your security settings is a proactive measure to safeguard your computerized character and individual data in an undeniably associated world. By assuming command over your internet-based protection settings, you can limit the dangers related to online cooperation and partake in a more secure and safer computerized insight.

Rehearsing Safe Web-based Conduct

The web has changed how we convey, work, and access data. While it offers various advantages, it additionally takes a chance connected with online dangers, security breaches, and cyberattacks. Rehearsing safe web-based conduct is significant to safeguard your computerized character, individual data, and generally online security. In this article, we will investigate fundamental ways to remain protected on the web.

1. Utilize Solid, Special Passwords:

Make solid and complex passwords that incorporate a mix of upper and lower-case letters, numbers, and extraordinary characters.

Try not to utilize effectively guessable data like names, birthday events, or well-known phrases.

Utilize an alternate secret phrase for each web-based record to keep a solitary break from compromising different records.

Think about utilizing a legitimate secret phrase chief to produce, store, and autofill your passwords safely.

2. Empower Two-Component Validation (2FA):

Whenever the situation allows, empower 2FA for your web-based accounts. This adds a layer of safety by expecting you to give a second verification technique (e.g., an instant message code or a biometric examination) notwithstanding your secret word.

3. Be Careful about Phishing Endeavors:

Be mindful of spontaneous messages, messages, or connections, particularly those mentioning individual data or login accreditations.

Check the validity of messages or messages from obscure shippers before tapping on joins or downloading connections.

Drift your mouse over connections to review the objective URL and check for irregularities or incorrect spellings.

4. Keep Programming and Gadgets Refreshed:

Routinely update your working framework, applications, and antivirus programming to fix security weaknesses.

Empower programmed refreshes when accessible to guarantee you get the most recent security fixes expeditiously.

5. Safeguard Your Data:

Be mindful about sharing individual data web-based, including your complete name, address, telephone number, and monetary subtleties.

Change the security settings via online entertainment stages to restrict how much private data is noticeable to other people.

Use pen name epithets when conceivable to safeguard your character.

6. Teach Yourself About Internet-based Tricks:

Remain informed about normal web-based tricks, for example, phishing, advance-expense extortion, and lottery tricks.

Have some doubts about offers that appear to be unrealistic or require forthright installments or individual data.

7. Utilize Secure Wi-Fi Organizations:

Try not to utilize public Wi-Fi networks for delicate exercises like internet banking or shopping, as they may not be secure.

Utilize a virtual confidential organization (VPN) to encode your web association and safeguard your information while utilizing public organizations.

8. Consistently Back Up Your Information:

Make normal reinforcements of your significant documents and information to defend against information misfortune because of equipment disappointment or ransomware assaults.

Store reinforcements on disconnected or outer gadgets to keep them from being compromised in cyberattacks.

9. Pursue Safe Online Entertainment Routines:

Survey and change your virtual entertainment protection settings to control who can see your posts and individual data.

Be wary about tolerating companion or association demands from obscure people.

10. Practice Watchfulness with Downloads and Connections:

Just download records or open email connections from confided-in sources.

Filter records for malware utilizing trustworthy antivirus programming before opening them.

Rehearsing safe web-based conduct is fundamental in the present advanced age. By following these tips and staying watchful, you can safeguard your data, monetary resources, and computerized character from a great many web-based dangers and cyberattacks, guaranteeing a more secure and safer web-based insight.

Instructing Others about Web-based Entertainment Duplicity

Virtual entertainment trickiness has become progressively common in the present computerized scene, presenting huge dangers to people and networks. Instructing others about virtual entertainment trickiness isn't just pivotal for their well-being but also for the aggregate work to make a more secure and more educated internet-based climate. In this article, we will investigate the significance of teaching others about virtual entertainment trickiness and give common tips on the most proficient method to do so.

Why Teach Others about Virtual Entertainment Misdirection

Advancing Web-based Security: Instruction enables people to perceive and answer tricky works on, shielding them from tricks, cyberbullying, and fraud.

Fortifying Computerized Proficiency: Understanding web-based entertainment trickiness works on advanced education, empowering individuals to assess online substance and pursue informed choices.

Forestalling the Spread of Deception: Taught people are less inclined to succumb to and propagate misleading data, adding to a more precise and reliable web-based talk.

Building Strength Against Control: Instruction outfits people with the ability to distinguish close-to-home control and try not to be influenced by misleading stories.

Reasonable Ways to Teach Others about Web-based Entertainment Trickery

Open Discourse:

Participate in open and non-critical discussions about online entertainment trickery with companions, relatives, and partners.

Urge questions and conversations to encourage a culture of mindfulness and learning.

Share Genuine Models:

Utilize genuine stories and contextual analyses to represent the risks of online entertainment duplicity. Feature the outcomes and effects on people and networks.

Give Assets:

Share instructive articles, recordings, and instructive assets via web-based entertainment duplicity, network safety, and advanced proficiency.

Prescribe dependable sites and associations committed to online security.

Show Decisive Reasoning:

Advance decisive reasoning abilities by empowering people to scrutinize the validity and believability of online substance.

Stress the significance of reality taking a look at it before sharing data.

Protection Settings and Security:

Offer direction on changing protection settings via web-based entertainment stages to restrict openness to likely trickiness.

Show others fundamental network safety rehearses, like areas of strength for utilizing and empowering two-factor confirmation.

Distinguish Warnings:

Help other people perceive normal warnings of virtual entertainment trickiness, like spontaneous solicitations for individual data, strange ways of behaving, or unrealistic offers.

Computerized Proficiency Studios:

Coordinate or go to computerized education studios or online courses zeroed in via web-based entertainment misdirection and online security.

Energize schools, public venues, or associations to host such occasions.

Be a Good example:

Show others how it is done in your web-based conduct. Tell others the best way to utilize online entertainment dependably, the truth look at data, and try not to spread duplicity.

Screen Online Action:

For guardians and gatekeepers, watch out for your youngsters' internet-based exercises and teach them about the expected dangers of duplicity and cyberbullying.

Report Dubious Movement:

Support announcing dubious records or content to online entertainment stages or applicable specialists.

Clarify that detailing tricky ways of behaving is a capable activity.

Teaching others about virtual entertainment double-dealing is an essential move toward making a more secure and more educated internet-based local area. By sharing information, advancing decisive reasoning, and offering useful direction, we can engage people to safeguard themselves as well as other people from the dangers of duplicity and add to a safer computerized scene.

Chapter Five

Legitimate and Policing against Online Double Dealing

As online trickiness and cybercrimes keep on rising, legitimate and policing assume a basic part in tending to these dangers. Regulations and implementation endeavors are crucial for considering culprits responsible and safeguarding people and associations from different types of online trickery. In this article, we will investigate the legitimacy and policing pointed toward battling on the web duplicity.

Legitimate Structure for Fighting Internet-based Duplicity

Cybercrime Regulation:

Numerous nations have established explicit regulations focusing on cybercrimes, including those connected with online misdirection. These regulations condemn exercises, for example, hacking, wholesale fraud, phishing, and online misrepresentation.

Information Assurance Regulations:

Information insurance guidelines, like the European Association's Overall Information Security Guideline (GDPR), expect associations to protect people's very own data. Infringement can bring about serious punishments.

Purchaser Insurance Regulations:

Shopper security regulations address tricky promoting, unreasonable strategic approaches, and misrepresentation in web-based business. They give legitimate solutions for casualties of online duplicity.

Protected Innovation Regulations:

Licensed innovation regulations safeguard people and organizations from online double dealing including copyright encroachment, brand name infringement, and fake products.

Policing

Cybercrime Units:

Numerous policing have particular cybercrime units devoted to examining on web misdirection, hacking, and different cybercrimes.

Worldwide Participation:

Cybercrimes frequently cross worldwide lines. Policing teams up with partners in different nations to capture and arraign cybercriminals.

Computerized Legal Sciences:

Computerized measurable groups utilize progressed procedures to gather, dissect, and save advanced proof connected with online trickiness cases.

Detailing Stages:

Numerous nations have laid out internet detailing stages where people and associations can report cybercrimes, making it simpler for police to track and explore cases.

Challenges in Fighting Web-based Trickery

Jurisdictional Issues:

Deciding to ward in cybercrime cases including numerous nations can be perplexing, dialing back examinations and arraignment.

Namelessness and Encryption:

Culprits frequently use nameless instruments and encryption to conceal their character and exercises, making it provoking for police to follow and catch them.

Developing Strategies:

Cybercriminals persistently adjust their strategies to avoid location and anticipation endeavors, requiring continuous updates to legitimate structures and analytical procedures.

Asset Limitations:

Policing may confront asset limits, frustrating their capacity to explore and indict all cybercrimes.

Forestalling On the Web Trickery:

While legitimate and policing are fundamental, counteraction is similarly significant. People and associations can find proactive ways to safeguard themselves from online trickiness:

- Instruct oneself and workers about internet-based dangers and safe web-based conduct.

- Carry major areas of strength for out measures, including hearty passwords, normal programming refreshes, and dependable antivirus programming.

- Use multifaceted confirmation (MFA) to improve security.

- Remain informed about rising digital dangers and misleading strategies.

- Report dubious action to policing important specialists quickly.

Legitimate and policing are basic parts of the battle against online misdirection. While challenges continue, continuous endeavors to fortify legitimate structures, upgrade global participation, and foster cybercrime-battling capacities are fundamental to combatting this advancing danger. People and associations ought to likewise assume a functioning part in counteraction and answering to establish a more secure web-based climate for all.

Cooperative Endeavors to Battle Con artists

Tricksters and fraudsters have become progressively complex in their strategies, representing a huge danger to people, organizations, and networks around the world. To successfully battle tricksters, cooperative endeavors including different partners are significant. In this article, we will investigate the significance of cooperative methodologies and feature central members in the battle against tricksters.

Why Cooperative Endeavors Matter

Multi-layered Dangers: Tricksters utilize a great many strategies, from internet phishing tricks to telephone-based misrepresentation and Ponzi plans. Cooperative endeavors unite different abilities to completely handle these complex dangers.

Cross-Boundary Activities: Numerous tricksters work across global lines, making it provoking for individual wards to resolve the issue. Cooperation works with cross-line examinations and activities.

Data Sharing: Sharing data about con artist strategies, known fraudsters, and rising dangers assists different associations and people in remaining educated and more ready.

Asset Improvement: Coordinated effort permits associations to pool assets, including financing, innovation, and faculty, for more proficient and financially savvy hostile to trick drives.

Key Partners in Cooperative Endeavors

Policing:

Neighborhood, public, and global policing assume a focal part in researching and arraigning tricksters.

Particular units and cybercrime divisions center around handling web tricks and extortion.

Government Administrative Bodies:

Government offices authorize and uphold regulations and guidelines connected with misrepresentation and shopper security.

They may likewise give instructive assets and admonitions to the general population.

Monetary Organizations:

Banks and monetary establishments screen exchanges and report dubious exercises that might be connected to tricks.

They team up with policing freeze resources and examine false monetary exchanges.

Innovation Organizations:

Web-based entertainment stages, web crawlers, and online commercial centers should keep tricksters from taking advantage of their foundation.

They might carry out announcing frameworks and calculations to identify and eliminate deceitful substances.

Charitable Associations:

Charitable associations devoted to customer assurance, network protection, and online security offer assets, backing, and support.

They frequently team up with different partners to bring issues to light and battle tricks.

Instructive Foundations:

Instructive foundations give preparation and mindfulness projects to help people perceive and keep away from tricks.

They may likewise lead examination to more readily grasp trickster strategies.

Online protection Firms:

Network safety organizations create and give apparatuses, programming, and administrations to shield people and organizations from online tricks and cyberattacks.

They may likewise impart dangerous insight to different partners.

Local area Guard dog Gatherings:

Neighborhood people group associations and guard dog bunches assume a vital part in distinguishing and revealing tricks inside their networks.

They bring issues to light and work with answering to policing.

Worldwide Associations:

Worldwide bodies, like INTERPOL and Europol, advance worldwide collaboration in handling cross-line cybercrimes and tricks.

They work with data sharing and joint activities.

Cooperative Drives in real life:

"Activity Phish Phry": This coordinated effort between the FBI, the U.S. Secret Assistance, and Egyptian specialists effectively destroyed a global phishing ring liable for taking large numbers of dollars from ledgers.

Monetary Industry Administrative Power (FINRA): FINRA teams up with monetary foundations to battle deceitful venture conspires and instruct financial backers about likely tricks.

Misrepresentation Watch Organization: AARP's Extortion Watch Organization teaches more seasoned grown-ups about tricks and teams up with policing to explore and indict fraudsters focusing on seniors.

The battle against con artists is a continuous fight that requires the aggregate endeavors of different partners. Cooperative drives and data sharing are fundamental for remaining one stride in front of fraudsters and shielding people and networks from the monetary and profound damage brought about by tricks. By cooperating, we can establish a more secure web and disconnected climate for everybody.

Remaining Cautious and Strong in the Advanced Age

The computerized age has achieved striking headways in innovation and networks. However, it has additionally presented new difficulties and dangers. Remaining careful and versatile in this period is fundamental to safeguarding yourself, your data, and your advanced personality. In this article, we will investigate the significance of carefulness and strength in the computerized age and give useful hints to assist you with exploring the advanced scene securely.

Why Stay Careful and Versatile

Online Dangers: The web is overflowing with dangers, including cyberattacks, tricks, fraud, and deception. Remaining watchful aides, you perceive and moderate these dangers.

Security Concerns: Your data is significant to both real organizations and pernicious entertainers. Carefulness guarantees you're mindful of how your information is gathered, utilized, and secured.

Data Overburden: In the time of data, it's pivotal to fundamentally assess the substance you experience online to recognize dependable data and falsehood.

Network safety: Cyberattacks can have extreme results, from monetary misfortune to information breaks. Being careful about network safety safeguards your computerized resources and online records.

Reasonable Ways to remain Careful and Versatile

Teach Yourself:

Remain informed about the most recent web-based dangers and tricks.

Focus on working on your computerized proficiency to more readily figure out internet-based chances and defensive measures.

Utilize Solid, Extraordinary Passwords:

Make solid passwords for your internet-based records and utilize an alternate secret phrase for each record.

Consider utilizing a secret word director to safely produce and store complex passwords.

Empower Two-Element Confirmation (2FA):

Turn on 2FA at whatever point conceivable to add a layer of safety to your records.

Watch Your Data:

Be mindful of sharing individual data on the web, particularly via virtual entertainment stages.

Change security settings to restrict who can get to your information.

Remain Incredulous:

Question the genuineness and validity of online substance, particularly if it appears to be unrealistic or excessively exciting.

Reality takes a look at data before sharing it, and be careful about misleading content titles.

Be careful with Phishing Endeavors:

Be mindful of spontaneous messages, messages, or connections, particularly those requesting individual data.

Check the source's personality and the authenticity of the solicitation.

Routinely Update Programming:

Keep your working framework, programming, and antivirus programs exceptional to fix weaknesses.

Secure Your Gadgets:

Set areas of strength for up-locks (PIN, secret phrase, unique mark, facial acknowledgment) on your gadgets to forestall unapproved access.

Introduce respectable security applications and empower gadget encryption.

Utilize a Virtual Confidential Organization (VPN):

Think about utilizing a VPN to scramble your web association, safeguarding your information from meddlesome eyes, particularly while utilizing public Wi-Fi organizations.

Back-Up Your Information:

Make standard reinforcements of significant records and information to safeguard against information misfortune because of equipment disappointments or ransomware assaults.

Report Dubious Action:

If you experience online dangers, tricks, or cyberbullying, report them to pertinent specialists or stages speedily.

Practice Advanced Detox:

Enjoy reprieves from the advanced world to lessen screen time and keep up with your psychological and profound prosperity.

Remaining cautious and strong in the computerized age is a proactive way to deal with defending your advanced character and individual data. By instructing yourself, utilizing solid network safety rehearses, and keeping a basic mentality, you can explore the computerized scene with certainty, safeguard your advanced resources, and add to a more secure and safer web-based climate.